ALEX AND THE GIANT STONE

AuthorHouse™
1663 Liberty Drive
Bloomington, IN 47403
www.authorhouse.com
Phone: 1 (800) 839-8640

Published by AuthorHouse 02/22/2019

ISBN: 978-1-7283-0096-2 (sc)
ISBN: 978-1-7283-0097-9 (e)
ISBN: 978-1-7283-0095-5 (hc)

Library of Congress Control Number: 2019901951

Print information available on the last page.

This book is printed on acid-free paper.

authorHOUSE®

ALEX AND THE GIANT STONE

MARIA CONSTANZA AGUILAR

Did you know that in a small town in Colombia there is a giant rock? Yes! There is a massive rock called El Peñon de Guatape, which is Spanish for the Crag of Guatape.

Let's go check it out and learn more about it!

The gigantic rock is visible from almost anywhere in town. It is so tall that even the tallest trees surrounding it look small in comparison.

The rock is over 650 feet (two hundred meters) tall and weighs ten million tons. The rock was naturally formed approximately seventy million years ago and is mainly composed of quartz, feldspar, and mica minerals.

The gigantic rock is located near the border of two towns, Guatape and El Peñol.

Guatape and El Peñol are both approximately two hours away from Medellin by car.

The rock is surrounded by a beautiful large lake and lots of plants and trees, which add even more beauty to the lake, the rock, and the view of the entire valley.

The magnificent lake can fully be seen from the top of the gigantic rock. There you can admire the glamorous view of the green water and plantations.

The lake has a breathtaking story. There is an entire town submerged beneath the surface. Originally the town of El Peñol was located at the bottom of the lake, but it was relocated to higher ground. The old town was flooded, and the only structures that survived the massive flood were the doctor's house, which has been turned into a museum, and the cross of the town's church.

Flooded? Yes, intentionally flooded during the construction of a huge hydroelectric dam that provides energy to many different parts of Colombia and neighboring countries, such as Ecuador, Peru, and Panama.

It is believed that more than four hundred thousand tourists visit the stone each year. The good news is that there are over thirty hotels in the area.

It is easy and simple to get to El Peñon de Guatape. You can either drive your own car, because it is easily accessible on well-maintained roads, or you can catch a bus or a taxi. There are also tourism companies that will offer packages and transportation to the stone.

There are many different restaurants in the area that provide authentic Colombian food. The most delicious is the famous fish, which is sure to make your mouth water. You cannot visit El Peñon de Guatape without trying their different fish dishes.

There are many fun and amazing things you can do during your visit to the massive stone. First and most importantly, you can climb the 659 steps to near the top of the stone.

Once you reach the top of the giant rock, you will find a souvenir shop where you can buy souvenirs for family and friends and even delicious authentic goodies from the region.

If you are feeling really energetic during your visit to the stone, you might as well continue climbing until you reach the very, very top—that's a total of 740 stairs. What a great feeling of accomplishment! Then you can sit back, relax, and enjoy a refreshing drink from the refreshment stand at the very top.

Wow! Amazing! What a great view! You can now enjoy the 360-degree view.

Once you are done climbing the stone you can take an exciting boat ride along the beautiful green waters. The tour guide will provide you with information about the stone, the lake, the flooded old Peñol, and the new Peñol, and will take you to visit the only house that survived the flooding, the museum.

There are also larger boats that can take you for a ride along the beautiful water. These larger boats do not have any stops. Instead they take you on a fun ride with nice music, which provides you the opportunity to sing and dance while you enjoy the ride and the view. You can also enjoy a helicopter ride, jet ski rides, water skiing and many more water sports.

You cannot leave El Peñon de Guatape without enjoying the excitement of the zip line, which will allow you a final view of the beautiful lake as you ride above its green water.

I only got to spend one day here at El Peñon de Guatape, but I enjoyed it so much that I would love to come back to this magnificent place and walk around the colorful streets!

Printed in the United States
By Bookmasters